A POCKET GUIDE TO SCOTTISH WORDS & PHRASES

So you don't look stupid
when trying to understand
the Edinburgh accent

PREFACE

Edinburgh is well known for the Scottish accent but for people from outside of the region, the dialect sounds friendly but foreign. It has an instantly recognisable and almost incomprehensible language. This mini illustrated 'dictionary' of Edinburgh words, sayings and explanations is here to rescue you.

AYE!

A DOIN

Beat someone in a fight.

"He gave Nathan a doin yesterday."

ABOOT

About.

"What ye talking aboot?"

AWA AN BILE YER HEID

Away and boil your head. In simple terms, go away.

"You don't know what you're talking aboot. Awa' an bile yer heid now."

AYE

Yes.

"Emma said aye to a kiss behind the shed."

AYE RIGHT

Expressing disbelief.

"Emma said that? Aye right."

BAFFIES

Slippers.

"These baffies are so cosy and warm."

BALTIC

Very cold.

"It's baltic out the day, I need my baffies."

BAMPOT

Idiot.

"The bampot Nathan messaged me again."

BANTER

Lively, humerous chat.

"We were having banter all day."

BARRY

To describe something good.

"That concert at Edinburgh Playhouse was barry."

BAWBAG

Literally, ball bag. Or idiot.

"You're such a bawbag pal."

B'EN

Location of an item.

"The teddy b'en on the bed."

BIRD

A girl or girlfriend.

"Say hello to my new bird, Emma."

BIT

House OR an area you are from.

"Meet me at ma bit tonight."

BLETHER

Catching up, gossiping or just talking for extended time periods.

"Let's have a blether over a cup of tea."

BOAK

Sick.

"*Nathan stunk, it was geein me the boak.*"

BOWFIN'

Disgusting, horrible

"Your socks are pure bowfin'."

BRAW

Brilliant, excellent, fantastic.

"The view from my window is braw."

BUCKET

Rubbish bin.

"Throw that piece in the bucket."

BUNKER

Kitchen worktop.

"Are you blind? The toaster is on the bunker."

BUZZIN'

Happy, excited. Having a good time.

"This place is brilliant, I'm buzzin'."

CHANCER

Someone who chances their luck.

"Stop bumming my cigarettes and buy your own you chancer."

CHEBS

Breasts.

"Emma is ugly but she has great chebs!"

CHORE

Steal.

"Did Nathan chore that watch?"

CHUM

To accompany.

*"I'll chum you to the shops so nobody
chores your watch."*

CLOSE

An alleyway.

"Let's take a shortcut down that close."

CLUDGIE

Toilet.

"I need a cludgie before we go the shop."

COLLIE BUCKIE

Piggy back.

"My feet hurt, gies a collie buckie home."

COORIE IN

Snuggle up.

"It was so cold, we corried in."

DAFTY

Stupid, silly or foolish.

"Stop pulling that face you dafty."

DEEK

To have a quick look at
something.

"Have a deek at that lass."

DINGHIED

Ignored someone.

"Emma dinghied me as I walked past."

DINNAE

Don't.

"*The sun is making its annual appearance. Dinnae forget your sunglasses.*"

DONE A BUNK

Flee a situation.

"The wallet was missing and Nathan has done a bunk! Suspicious."

DREEP

Descend from a height by dangling.

"We're going to have to dreep down the window."

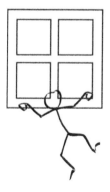

DREICH

Wet, grey and gloomy weather.

"It's another surprisingly dreich day outside today."

EDGY

Keeping a watch whilst getting up to no good.

"I'll keep the edgy while you sneak in."

EEJIT

A friendly harmless idiot.

"Check that eejit over there."

EMBRA

Local pronunciation of Edinburgh, the Athens of the north.

"Embra Castle is better than the Acropolis."

FEART

Used to express fear.

"*I'm feart to go on the plane, I don't like flying.*"

FIZZY JUICE

A soft drink. Pop or soda.

"I need a bottle of fizzy juice."

GALLUS

Acting daring or boldly.

"The way Nathan spoke to Emma was gallus."

GEEZ

Give me.

"Geez the remote, Shetland is starting."

GEN UP

Honestly.

"I saw a spaceship, gen up."

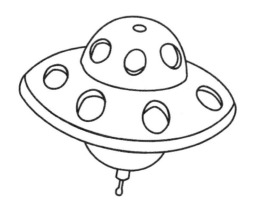

GET TAE

Used to tell someone to go away.

"Get tae f*ck Nathan."

GREET

Cry.

"It wasn't funny, I was pure greetin'."

GROWLIN'

Give a dirty look to express dislike for someone.

"What's his problem growlin' at us."

HACKET

An ugly person.

"Nathan's new bird is hacket."

HAPPENIN'

Used as a greeting to ask how you are.

"Happenin' pal, haven't seen you for a long time?"

HAUD YER WEESHT

Used to tell someone to shut up.

"Haud yer weesht before I make you."

HAVNAE A SCOOBY

I haven't got a clue.

"What time is it?"
"I havnae a scooby."

HEAVY RAGIN'

Used when very angry.

"Emma was heavy ragin' like a mad frog."

HOACHIN'

Busy OR in desperate need of something.

"The pub was mobbed today but we still waited as I was hoachin' for a drink."

JESSIE

Wimp, wuss or scaredy cat.

"Don't be such a Jessie."

JOBBY

Poo.

"You canny polish a jobby."

KEN

Know.

"I ken that man."

KNOCK OFF

Fake designer clothes.

"Your trainers are knock offs."

LUMBER

Date.

"I have a lumber so I won't be going to the dance on my own."

MESSAGES

Food shopping.

"Nathan is getting the messages."

MUNTER

Ugly person.

"That's Emma, she's a munter."

NASH

Run away or move fast.

"It's starting to rain, lets nash."

NED

Non Educated Delinquent.
Scottish equivalent of a chav.

"Ay I'm no a NED."

NUMPTY

Endearing term for an idiot.

"The numpty is sleep driving."

PATTER

Banter, chat.

"Emma was a hacket but I got off with her because her patter was excellent."

PEELY-WALLY

Pale, off colour. Looking unwell.

"Nathan had the flu and was looking a bit peely-wally."

PIE

Ignore someone on purpose.

"Nathan just got pied."

PIECE

Sandwich.

"I'm getting my piece from the fridge."

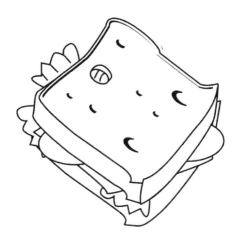

PISH

A word to describe something not good.

"What's the weather like?"
"Raining cats and dogs, pure pish man."

PURE

Really or a lot.

"Scotland is pure class."

RANK

Disgusting.

"That smell is rank."

REEKING

Intoxicated, drunk, out of it.

"We went into town last night and Nathan was absolutely reeking!"

RIDDY

Feeling embarrassed, red face.

"Emma was riddy when she let one off."

RIPS MA KNITTIN'

Annoys.

"That pure rips ma knittin' when people stop right in front of you."

SAUCE

Mixture of vinegar and brown sauce from the chippy.

"Plenty of salt and sauce on that please."

SHAN

Unfair or disappointing.

"My boss was so mad today, well shan."

SKELP

Slap.

"If you don't behave yourself you'll be skelped."

SKOOSH

Fizzy drink.

"Giz a bottle of skoosh."

SOOK

Person who sucks up to someone.

"You told the boss you liked her shoes, you're such a sook."

SOUND

Cool, good, brilliant, fantastic, great, ace, wonderful.

"Nathan was sound."

SQUARE GO

The Scottish call to fight.

"You're pis*ing me off, square go the now!"

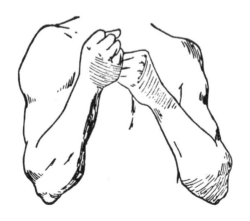

STEAMIN'

Drunk.

"Emma was steamin' last night."

STOOSHIE

A minor spat or fight.

"There was a stooshie at the pub but it didn't last long."

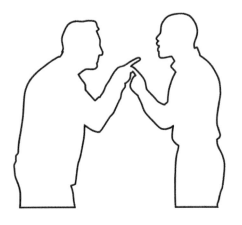

SWATCH

Have a brief look at.

"Geez a swatch at your new glasses."

THE DAY

Today.

"Having a great time reading this the day."

WALLIES

False teeth, dentures.

"I'll give you the need to get wallies if you don't watch yourself."

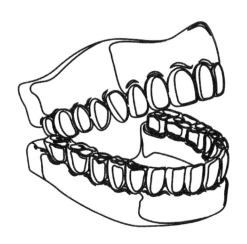

WARMER

Used to describe someone who gets on your nerves.

"Nathan's sister is a pure warmer!"

WINCH

Kiss.

"Gees a winch before I say goodbye."

PURE CLASS
PURE CLASS
PURE CLASS
PURE CLASS
PURE CLASS
PURE CLASS
PURE CLASS
PURE CLASS
PURE CLASS
PURE CLASS
PURE CLASS